BROADWAY FAVORITES

Solos and Band Arrangements
Correlated with Essential Elements Band Me[...]

Arranged by
MICHAEL SWEENEY

Welcome to Essential Elements Broadway Favorites! There are two versions of each selection in this versatile book. The SOLO version appears in the beginning of each student book. The FULL BAND arrangements of each song follows. The supplemental CD recording or PIANO ACCOMPANIMENT BOOK may be used as an accompaniment for solo performance. Use these recordings when playing solos for friends and family.

ISBN 978-0-7935-9846-5

HAL•LEONARD®
CORPORATION
7777 W. BLUEMOUND RD. P.O. BOX 13819 MILWAUKEE, WI 53213

00860040

From Walt Disney's BEAUTY AND THE BEAST: THE BROADWAY MUSICAL

BEAUTY AND THE BEAST

Bb **Bass Clarinet**
Solo

Lyrics by HOWARD ASHMAN
Music by ALAN MENKEN
Arranged by MICHAEL SWEENEY

00860040

From the Musical Production ANNIE
TOMORROW

Lyric by MARTIN CHARNIN
Music by CHARLES STROUSE
Arranged by MICHAEL SWEENEY

Bb BASS CLARINET
Solo

00860040

From the Musical CABARET
CABARET

Words by FRED EBB
Music by JOHN KANDER
Arranged by MICHAEL SWEENEY

B♭ **BASS CLARINET**
Solo

From THE SOUND OF MUSIC
EDELWEISS

Lyrics by OSCAR HAMMERSTEIN II
Music by RICHARD RODGERS
Arranged by MICHAEL SWEENEY

B♭ BASS CLARINET
Solo

00860040

From EVITA

DON'T CRY FOR ME ARGENTINA

Bb BASS CLARINET
Solo

Words by TIM RICE
Music by ANDREW LLOYD WEBBER
Arranged by MICHAEL SWEENEY

MCA Music Publishing

GET ME TO THE CHURCH ON TIME

Bb BASS CLARINET
Solo

Words by ALAN JAY LERNER
Music by FREDERICK LOEWE
Arranged by MICHAEL SWEENEY

From LES MISÉRABLES

I DREAMED A DREAM

Music by CLAUDE-MICHEL SCHÖNBERG
Lyrics by ALAIN BOUBLIL,
JEAN-MARC NATEL and HERBERT KRETZMER
Arranged by MICHAEL SWEENEY

B♭ BASS CLARINET
Solo

Music and French Lyrics Copyright © 1980 by Editions Musicales Alain Boublil
English Lyrics Copyright © 1986 by Alain Boublil Music Ltd. (ASCAP)
This edition Copyright © 1998 by Alain Boublil Music Ltd. (ASCAP)
Mechanical and Publication Rights for the U.S.A. Administered by Alain Boublil Music Ltd. (ASCAP)
c/o Spielman Koenigsberg & Parker LLP, Richard Koenigsberg, 1745 Broadway, New York NY 10019, Tel 212-453-2500, Fax 212-453-2550, ABML@skpny.com

From JOSEPH AND THE AMAZING TECHNICOLOR DREAMCOAT
GO GO GO JOSEPH

Bb BASS CLARINET
Solo

Music by ANDREW LLOYD WEBBER
Lyrics by TIM RICE
Arranged by MICHAEL SWEENEY

00860040

From CATS
MEMORY

B♭ BASS CLARINET
Solo

Music by ANDREW LLOYD WEBBER
Text by TREVOR NUNN after T.S. ELIOT
Arranged by MICHAEL SWEENEY

THE PHANTOM OF THE OPERA

Bb BASS CLARINET
Solo

Music by ANDREW LLOYD WEBBER
Lyrics by CHARLES HART
Additional Lyrics by RICHARD STILGOE and MIKE BATT
Arranged by MICHAEL SWEENEY

From Meredith Willson's THE MUSIC MAN

SEVENTY SIX TROMBONES

Bb **BASS CLARINET**

SOLO

By MEREDITH WILLSON
Arranged by MICHAEL SWEENEY

00860040

BEAUTY AND THE BEAST

Bb BASS CLARINET
Band Arrangement

Lyrics by HOWARD ASHMAN
Music by ALAN MENKEN
Arranged by MICHAEL SWEENEY

From the Musical Production ANNIE

TOMORROW

Bᵇ **BASS CLARINET**
Band Arrangement

Lyric by MARTIN CHARNIN
Music by CHARLES STROUSE
Arranged by MICHAEL SWEENEY

00860040

CABARET

From the Musical CABARET

Words by FRED EBB
Music by JOHN KANDER
Arranged by MICHAEL SWEENEY

B♭ BASS CLARINET
Band Arrangement

00860040

From THE SOUND OF MUSIC
EDELWEISS

B♭ **BASS CLARINET**
BAND Arrangement

Lyrics by OSCAR HAMMERSTEIN II
Music by RICHARD RODGERS
Arranged by MICHAEL SWEENEY

DON'T CRY FOR ME ARGENTINA

Bb **BASS CLARINET**
Band Arrangement

Words by TIM RICE
Music by ANDREW LLOYD WEBBER
Arranged by MICHAEL SWEENEY

00860040

MCA Music Publishing

From MY FAIR LADY

GET ME TO THE CHURCH ON TIME

B♭ BASS CLARINET
Band Arrangement

Words by ALAN JAY LERNER
Music by FREDERICK LOEWE
Arranged by MICHAEL SWEENEY

00860040

From LES MISÉRABLES

I DREAMED A DREAM

Bb BASS CLARINET
Band Arrangement

Music by CLAUDE-MICHEL SCHÖNBERG
Lyrics by ALAIN BOUBLIL,
JEAN-MARC NATEL and HERBERT KRETZMER
Arranged by MICHAEL SWEENEY

From JOSEPH AND THE AMAZING TECHNICOLOR DREAMCOAT

GO GO GO JOSEPH

B♭ BASS CLARINET
Band Arrangement

Music by ANDREW LLOYD WEBBER
Lyrics by TIM RICE
Arranged by MICHAEL SWEENEY

00860040

From CATS
MEMORY

B♭ BASS CLARINET
Band Arrangement

Music by ANDREW LLOYD WEBBER
Text by TREVOR NUNN after T.S. ELIOT
Arranged by MICHAEL SWEENEY

00860040

From THE PHANTOM OF THE OPERA

THE PHANTOM OF THE OPERA

B♭ BASS CLARINET
Band Arrangement

Music by ANDREW LLOYD WEBBER
Lyrics by CHARLES HART
Additional Lyrics by RICHARD STILGOE and MIKE BATT
Arranged by MICHAEL SWEENEY

00860040

From Meredith Willson's THE MUSIC MAN

SEVENTY SIX TROMBONES

By MEREDITH WILLSON
Arranged by MICHAEL SWEENEY

Bb BASS CLARINET
Band Arrangement

00860040